Franesca. 5

No Entry

Jan Carew

Stanley Thornes (Publishers) Ltd

First published in 1985 by Hutchinson Education
Reprinted in 1986, 1988, 1989

Reprinted in 1991 by
Stanley Thornes (Publishers) Ltd
Old Station Drive
Leckhampton
CHELTENHAM GL53 0DN
England

British Library Cataloguing in Publication Data
Carew, Jan
  No Entry.—(Spirals)
  1. Readers—1950-
  I. Title
  428.6   PE1119

ISBN 0 7487 1044 2

Cover illustration by Simon Rees
Cover design by Martin Grant-Hudson
Printed and bound in Great Britain at Martin's of Berwick

Contents

A complete list of Spirals

Stories

Jim Alderson
Crash in the Jungle
The Witch Princess

Jan Carew
Death Comes to the Circus

Susan Duberley
The Ring

**Keith Fletcher and
Susan Duberley**
Nightmare Lake

John Goodwin
Dead-end Job

Paul Groves
Not that I'm Work-shy
The Third Climber

Anita Jackson
The Actor
The Austin Seven
Bennet Manor
Dreams
The Ear
A Game of Life or Death
No Rent to Pay

Paul Jennings
Eye of Evil
Maggot

Margaret Loxton
The Dark Shadow

Patrick Nobes
Ghost Writer

Kevin Philbin
Summer of the Werewolf

John Townsend
Beware of the Morris Minor
Fame and Fortune
SOS

David Walke
Dollars in the Dust

Plays

Jan Carew
Computer Killer
No Entry
Time Loop

John Godfrey
When I Count to Three

Nigel Gray
An Earwig in the Ear

Paul Groves
Tell Me Where it Hurts

Barbara Mitchelhill
Punchlines
The Ramsbottoms at Home

Madeline Sotheby
Hard Times at Batwing Hall

John Townsend
Cheer and Groan
The End of the Line
Hanging by a Fred
The Lighthouse Keeper's Secret
Making a Splash
Murder at Muckleby Manor
Over and Out
Taking the Plunge

David Walke
The Bungle Gang Strikes Again
The Good, the Bad and the Bungle
Package Holiday

No Entry

8 parts:
Peter Evans, Molly Evans, Mrs Jones, Ron Barker, Mary Barker, Basher Bates, Fingers Flanagan, Policeman

Scene 1 Peter and *Molly Evans* are in the kitchen of their house. It is tea-time.

Molly [*Susan*]   Well, Peter [*Dad*]. How did your driving lesson go?

Peter   Very badly, I'm afraid. I don't think I'll ever make a driver, love. I hate to let you down but. . . .

Molly   Nonsense, Peter! Of course you'll learn to drive. Everyone does. And just think how useful it will be. To carry home the shopping and have days out in the country – oh, it'll be lovely! Now that I've hurt my leg, I can't drive for a while. And I do miss the car. We really need you to learn, Peter.

Peter   Yes, but don't count on it. After today, I don't think I ever want to get into a car again.

5

Molly	But what went wrong?
Peter	A lot of things. Or so the driving teacher said. He wasn't a very nice man. And I don't think he liked me, Molly.
Molly	What made you think that, ~~Peter?~~ *Dad*
Peter	Oh, just something he said as I got out of the car.
Molly	What was it?
Peter	He said he'd give up a whole week's wages if I went to another driving school. That wasn't very nice was it?
Molly	No, it wasn't. What a horrid thing to say! I mean, everyone has to learn.
Peter	That's what I thought. Anyway, I think I *will* try another driving school.
Molly	What about that new one – the Easy Drive School in Bruce Street?
Peter	Yes, I may try a lesson with them.
	[*Voice is heard off-stage*]
Mrs Jones	Hello! Are you there, Mrs Evans?
Molly	[*In a low voice*] Oh Lord! It's that nosy neighbour, Mrs Jones. I can't stand her. She's always dropping in for a chat. And

she's such a show-off! Always bragging about how well-off they are. [*In a louder voice*] Yes, Mrs Jones. We're in the kitchen. We've just finished tea.

[Mrs Jones *comes in*]

Mrs Jones   Hello, Mrs E. Hello, Mr E. How are you? Well, I hope.

Peter   Yes, we're fine.

Mrs Jones   How did your driving lesson go?

Peter   How did *you* know I was learning?

Mrs Jones   A little bird told me. How did your lesson go? Not very well, I believe.

Molly   What makes you think that?

Mrs Jones   It's not easy when you start. Everyone knows that.

Peter   Thanks a lot. I've been learning for six weeks already.

Mrs Jones   And that old banger of yours – well, it's not the best car to learn in, is it? What a pity you can't afford a new one!

Molly   Oh, I don't know. We like our old car. It'll do fine for now. And as for Peter's lesson – it went very well. Didn't it, dear?

7

Mrs Jones	Oh, that's funny. My husband, Bert, saw the driving teacher at the end of the lesson. He was mopping his face with his hanky and looked white as a sheet.
Peter	And how did Bert see that?
Mrs Jones	He just happened to be driving past in his new car. Haven't you seen it yet? It's lovely! So big and comfortable. Well, I mustn't stop. I've got a lot to do before we go out tonight. Bert's taking me to dinner at that new restaurant. You know – the posh French one. It looks very expensive. But that doesn't bother Bert.
Peter	No. It wouldn't.
Mrs Jones	Well, I must go. Goodbye for now.

Scene 2

Molly	Doesn't that woman make you sick?
Peter	Her husband's even worse. A real handyman. I hate it when he asks you if we want any jobs done in the house, Molly. As if we couldn't do jobs. I mean – I built those shelves in the kitchen, didn't I?
Molly	Yes, dear. They were lovely shelves. It

Susan

8

was a pity they fell down when you put anything on them.

| Peter | That was the fault of the wall. How was I to know the wall was weak? |

| Molly | Yes, dear. And it was a pity the neighbours got to know about the time we were knee-deep in water. Remember? It was when you mended that loose floorboard. |

| Peter | I wasn't to know there was a water pipe under the floor. |

| Molly | No, dear. Never mind! You go and book a lesson with the Easy Drive School. I bet your next lesson will go just fine! |

Scene 3 Ron Barker of the Easy Drive School, is giving *Peter Evans* a lesson.

| Ron | Now, Mr Evans, don't be scared. It's only a car. It won't bite you. How many lessons have you had? |

| Peter | Six. With that other driving school. But I'm not going there again. |

| Ron | Why is that, Mr Evans? |

| Peter | The man shouted at me. How can I drive if people shout at me? |

Ron	Quite right. I never shout at my pupils. At least, not often. Er – why did the teacher shout at you? Any special reason?
Peter	It was at a roundabout.
Ron	Ah yes! Perhaps you didn't slow down when you got to the roundabout. You must give way to traffic from the right, you know, Mr Evans.
Peter	It wasn't that.
Ron	No?
Peter	No, I remember now. I knew there was something wrong when I got onto the roundabout.
Ron	What made you think that, Mr Evans?
Peter	All the other drivers were hooting their horns and shaking their fists. That was when I knew.
Ron	Knew what?
Peter	I was driving round the roundabout the wrong way. That was why the teacher shouted.
Ron	I-I see. Yes, that was a bit risky. Well, we won't do anything like that today, will we, Mr Evans?

Peter	I hope not. It all depends.
Ron	Depends on what?
Peter	The other traffic.
Ron	What do you mean?
Peter	If the other cars would just keep away from me, everything would be all right.
Ron	Yes, well, I think we'll start driving. This is your own car, isn't it? Now just turn the key and start the engine. [Peter *does it*] There, that wasn't difficult, was it? You're doing fine. Now before you start driving, what do you do?
Peter	Do?
Ron	Yes, you always have to do something before you drive off. What did your other teacher tell you to do?
Peter	He asked me to remember that he was the father of a family and didn't want to die just yet.
Ron	No, that wasn't what I meant. I was thinking of looking in the mirror. You always check your mirror before you drive off. Now, just look in the mirror. What do you see?
Peter	Goodness!

Ron	What is it?
Peter	Just look at those trees against the sky. If only I had my camera with me.
Ron	Mr Evans, it isn't *trees* I want you to look for. It's cars! Is the road clear of cars behind you?
Peter	Yes.
Ron	Then drive off.
Peter	There seems to be something wrong.
Ron	Yes, Mr Evans. We're going backwards. You've gone into reverse gear by mistake. Stop and try once more.
Peter	OK. How's that?
Ron	You're doing fine now, Mr Evans. Keep well to the left, that's right. There, that isn't so bad, is it? I don't know what your other teacher was going on about. You're doing just fine. Er – I'd slow down a bit if I were you, Mr Evans. You're going a little too fast. This is a built-up area. Please use the brake, Mr Evans. MR EVANS, SLOW DOWN!
Peter	All right, all right. There's no need to shout. I'm not deaf, you know. I just got mixed up for a minute. They look so alike.

Ron	What do?
Peter	All these pedals. There are three of them after all. I forgot the brake was the one in the middle. It's a pity they have to be so close together.
Ron	Yes, isn't it? That's the way cars are made, I'm afraid. Shall we try again?

Scene 4 The Easy Drive office. *Ron* comes in.

Ron	Gosh! Am I glad to be back in one piece!
~~Mary~~ *Jane*	What do you mean, Ron?
Ron	That Mr Evans! I ought to take out extra life insurance when I drive with him. He's not a learner driver, he's an act of God. You feel every minute is going to be your last.
~~Mary~~ *Jane*	Oh, come on. He can't be that bad. He probably doesn't like machines. A lot of people don't.
Ron	It isn't machines he has a thing against. I reckon it's driving teachers.
~~Mary~~ *Jane*	He might get on better with a woman teacher. ~~I'll~~ *Let Mary* take him out next time.
Ron	You don't know what you're in for, Mary.

13

	I hope you've made your will, that's all I can say.
~~Mary~~ *Jane*	We have to teach Mr Evans. We don't have very many pupils.
Ron	Yes, I know. I don't know how long we'll be able to keep going, ~~Mary.~~ The bank manager is getting a bit nasty about the money we borrowed.
~~Mary~~ *Jane*	But we need time to build up the business! I'm sure we'll get more pupils soon.
Ron	Let's hope so. But not like Mr Evans or we might not have a business left to build up. In fact, we might not even still be alive!
Mary	Oh, come on, Ron. He can't be that bad. You leave Mr Evans to me. I bet I'll make a driver out of him.

Scene 5 A week later.

Mary	Now, Mr Evans, don't be nervous.
Peter	Oh, I'm not nervous.
Mary	Aren't you? That's good. I wish I felt the same.
Peter	What?

14

Mary	Just a joke, Mr Evans. I can remember when I learned to drive. It's very hard at first, isn't it?
Peter	Well, yes, it is a bit. I thought it would help having driven a bumper car at the fair.
Mary	Oh no, it's not a bit like that. You must try not to hit anything. In bumper cars, that's half the fun. Well, shall we begin? Drive off when you're ready. Very good. Just keep to the left a bit more. That's fine.
Peter	Oh, that reminds me! I promised my wife I'd buy some fairy lights for our Christmas tree.
Mary	What reminds you?
Peter	Those pretty lights just ahead. They keep changing colour.
Mary	Mr Evans ... those are traffic lights! And they've just gone red! Mr Evans, STOP!! Just in time. There could have been a nasty accident. You really must stop at red lights, Mr Evans. Red means danger, remember.
Peter	Oh, dear. I'm sorry. My mind was far away. I'll never learn to drive.

Mary	Yes, you will, Mr Evans. Everyone learns in the end. As long as they live long enough, of course. But let's not flirt with death at the traffic lights again. I don't think my nerves could stand it.
Peter	All right. Where do we go now?
Mary	Just drive on till we come to the next junction. Now, you know what a junction is, don't you? Where two or more roads meet. We have to do something when we come to the junction. Do you know what it is?
Peter	[*Thinks*] I'm not sure.
Mary	Well, what did your other teacher do when you came to a junction?
Peter	Oh, now I remember.
Mary	Good!
Peter	Every time we came to a junction, he used to start praying. I think he was a Catholic.
Mary	No, that wasn't what I meant. You have to look right, then left, then right again before coming out of the junction. That's to make sure the road is clear. All right?
Peter	Right. I'll remember to look.

Mary	Just one more thing, Mr Evans. I know you're nervous but please don't duck behind the wheel every time you see a lorry. It doesn't do a lot for your driving. Remember, the other drivers are just as scared of you, as you are of them. [*Under her breath*] More, if they have any sense.
Peter	All right. I'll try.

Scene 6 An empty house nearby. *Basher Bates* and *Fingers Flanagan* are planning their next job. They are thieves.

Basher	Now listen Fingers, this plan can't fail.
Fingers	That's what you said last time, Basher. But I got two years in jail.
Basher	Yes, that was a pity. If only that nosy copper hadn't come along just then.
Fingers	It was more than a pity. He caught me red-handed with the stuff. And you got away!
Basher	Well, let's not think about the past. It's the present that counts. Now for my plan. Are you listening?
Fingers	OK – what is it?

Basher	You know that jewellery shop in Parry Road?
Fingers	What, that new one?
Basher	Yes, that's it. It's a very posh place with carpets and fancy lights. A real classy joint.
Fingers	I know the one. It's got really good stuff in the window.
Basher	And even better stuff inside. Gold, diamonds, emeralds, rubies – the lot.
Fingers	Don't Basher! You're making my mouth water and my fingers itch.
Basher	I knew you'd be keen. You aren't called Fingers for nothing.
Fingers	Oh, I'm keen all right. There's just one snag.
Basher	Yes?
Fingers	How can we get in there without being seen?
Basher	That, my boy, is where Basher has been really clever.
Fingers	Go on – I'm listening.
Basher	You know those little tents they have for road works? The men work inside and no-one can see what they're doing.

Fingers	That's so they can have a cup of tea when they want.
Basher	It doesn't matter why. It's just what we need. There's a manhole just outside the jewellery shop. We can put up the tent and tunnel under the shop. Then we can come up inside and help ourselves. The shop will have to be closed, of course.
Fingers	Sounds too good to be true. But what if someone comes along and asks us what we're doing?
Basher	No one will. I've not only got a little tent for us to work in. I've got something else as well. Believe me, Fingers, no one will bother us. We'll have the road to ourselves. What do you think?
Fingers	It might work, Basher. You seem to have thought of everything.
Basher	You bet I have. Just you wait and see, this plan can't fail.

Scene 7 Mary is again teaching *Peter* to drive. They have just driven off.

Peter	The car doesn't seem to be going very fast today. It feels a bit heavy – as if something were pulling it back.

Mary	You could try taking the handbrake off, Mr Evans.
Peter	Oh, is it still on? Goodness me, so it is. No wonder the car couldn't go properly.
Mary	No wonder. Take the next turning on the left. Don't forget to signal first. No, it's down for left, remember.
Peter	Why is that driver hooting behind me?
Mary	Never mind him, Mr Evans. It's just that you signalled right and then left. He wasn't sure where we were going. But don't worry. He had to learn once too.
Peter	Is this the turning?
Mary	That's right. You need a bit of practice in turning corners, Mr Evans. You must go more slowly.
Peter	Didn't I come round that corner all right?
Mary	Well, yes, except that you aren't supposed to hit the pavement. Didn't you feel the bump as you went round?
Peter	Oh, was that what the bump was? I did wonder. Oh dear!
Mary	Never mind. At least it wasn't a person. Now let's try another corner. Take the next turning on the left.

Peter	Here we go. Let's see if I do it right this time.
Mary	Wait, Mr Evans! We'd better not go down that road after all. Don't you see the sign? It says 'No Entry'. We'd better go straight on, Mr Evans. Mr Evans!!
Peter	Too late! I'm already turning the corner. I can't stop now.
Mary	But we must stop! We're breaking the Highway Code. There may be a good reason for the 'No Entry' sign. Oh heavens! Look out!
	[*There is a crashing noise as the car hits a workmen's tent in the road*]
	Now we've done it!
Peter	What was that noise? What have we hit?
Mary	We've hit the reason for the 'No Entry' sign. I only hope we haven't killed anybody. We'd better get out and see.
Peter	Oh Lord! Look who's coming now!
Mary	A policeman. Of course! They're never slow to turn up if there's an accident. Hello, officer.
Policeman 1	Hello, Madam. Had a spot of trouble, have you? I heard the crash.

21

Mary	My pupil had a little accident.
Policeman 1	Yes, I can see that. That workman's tent is a right mess. Where are the workmen? Is anybody hurt?
Mary	I don't know. We haven't seen anybody yet.
Policeman 2	That's funny. I didn't know there were road-works here today. They always tell the police things like that.
Peter	Oh dear, what will happen now? Will we have our names in the paper? Will we have to go to court?
Mary	I don't know yet. Maybe we haven't done much damage. I hope it will be OK. This could put Ron and me out of a job.
Peter	Oh Lord! I *am* sorry.
Mary	Perhaps you could learn your Highway Code, Mr Evans? Then next time you see a 'No Entry' sign, you'll know what it means.
Peter	I'll do my best.
Policeman 1	Hello, what have we here? I do believe it's two old friends of mine, climbing out of that hole in the ground. I'd know

those ugly faces anywhere. This is getting interesting. Hello, Basher, hello, Fingers. Doing a spot of digging, are we? I didn't know you'd gone into the road-mending business.

Basher   Oh no! It's Constable Brown.

Fingers   It wasn't my fault, Constable. It was all Basher's idea.

Policeman 1 Let's just take a walk down to the station, shall we? Then we'll sort it all out. What's that you're carrying? Those sacks look heavy. Let me carry them for you. No, no, I insist. Hand them over, boys. Now come along with me.

Mary   What about us, officer? What about the accident?

Policeman 2 Oh, I don't think we need to worry about that, madame. Looks like we've caught a couple of thieves, thanks to you.

[*He leaves with the two men*]

Mary   Well, Mr Evans. It looks as if everything is all right. We won't have to appear in court. Thank goodness for that. Do you mind if I drive us back home? Just in case we meet anything on the way.

Scene 8 The Easy Drive Office

Ron	Wonderful news, Mary.
Mary	What? Have we won the pools? *lottery*
Ron	No, not that. That little accident you had with Mr Evans – remember?
Mary	Could I ever forget?
Ron	The police opened the sacks those two men had. Guess what they found?
Mary	What?
Ron	Gold and jewels. They'd broken into the jeweller's shop and just about cleaned the place out.
Mary	So they *were* thieves!
Ron	They certainly were. And the jeweller is so grateful, he wants to pay a reward. The police told him it was the Easy Drive driving school who found the thieves. And we are now two thousand pounds richer! And so is Mr Evans. He's going to buy a decent car now, he says.
Mary	Great! So we can pay off our bank loan.
Ron	And we can advertise for new pupils. After all, we can't just teach Mr Evans all the time.

24

Mary	[*Laughs*] Oh, I don't know. He *is* a full-time job. But there's one good thing.
Ron	What's that?
Mary	At least he knows one of the road signs now.
Ron	Oh yes? Which one?
Mary	No Entry, of course!

Bed and Breakfast

7 parts:
Stella White, Bob White, Mr Baker, Mrs Baker,
Mr Potter-Smith, Mrs Potter-Smith, Cousin Ernest

Scene 1 Seaview Guest House. It's breakfast time
and *Mr* and *Mrs Baker* are at a table. *Mr* and
Mrs Potter-Smith come in. They are a very snooty
couple.

Mrs P-S	Good morning.
The Bakers	Good morning.
Mrs P-S	I see that breakfast is late again, is it?
Mrs Baker	No, we've just come down.
Mrs P-S	I must say I don't think much of this guest house. Do you, Geoffrey?
Mr P-S	No, my dear. It's not the sort of place we're used to.
Mrs P-S	We usually go to the Ritz Hotel, you know.
Mr Baker	Really? Why didn't you go this year? Couldn't you afford it?

Mr P-S	It wasn't a question of money. The hotel was already full.
Mrs P-S	So I'm afraid we had to come here. And I must say, this couple have no idea how to run a guest house.
Mrs Baker	Oh, I don't agree. Mr and Mrs White are new to the business but they do their best.
Mr Baker	Yes, they work very hard to look after us.
Mrs P-S	I suppose it all depends what you're used to.
Mr P-S	Yes. We are simply used to better things.
	[Stella White *comes in with a large tray. She is hot and flushed*]
Stella	Sorry, breakfast is a bit late today.
Mrs Baker	That's all right, Mrs White. We haven't been waiting long.
Stella	The toaster has gone funny again. I must have it fixed.
Mrs Baker	What's wrong with it, dear? Doesn't the toast pop up?
Stella	Oh, it pops up all right. In fact, it jumps

right across the kitchen. Most of it ended up on the floor.

Mrs P-S	Dear me! I hope that isn't the toast *we're* going to eat!
Stella	Don't worry, Mrs Potter-Smith. I did some fresh toast and managed to catch it as it flew through the air.
Mrs P-S	Geoffrey! Did you hear that? Toast flying through the air! What kind of place is this?
Mr Baker	[*Laughs*] Well done, Mrs White! You must be good at catching. Did you play rounders at school?
Mrs P-S	When you've quite finished your conversation, we'd like to have our breakfast, please. I only hope it's still hot enough to eat.
Mr P-S	Not cold like yesterday.
Mrs P-S	Or the day before.
Stella	I think you'll find it hot enough. Here you are.

[Stella *serves breakfast to all the guests*]

Scene 2 Breakfast is over and *Stella* is clearing the tables. *Bob* comes in.

Bob	Hello, love. I've got the car going at last, so we can use it for shopping today.
Stella	Thank goodness for that.
Bob	What's the matter, Stella? You look a bit low. Never mind, it's my turn to do breakfast tomorrow. Let me give you a hand with clearing those tables.
Stella	Thanks, love. I'm all right, really. But I never knew it was so hard to run a guest house. There's always so much to do!
Bob	We're new to it, remember! We'll get much better at it as time goes on.
Stella	I suppose so. It would be nice if we could afford some help, though. And if we could get the place fixed up properly. Things keep breaking down. Like that blasted toaster.
Bob	Don't tell me it broke down again! I fixed the spring so the toast would pop up.
Stella	Yes, Bob. Only you fixed it so well, the toast nearly hit the ceiling. In fact, one piece did hit the ceiling and I think it's still there.
Bob	Oh Lord! Sorry, Stella.

Stella	[*Laughs*] Never mind. It's funny, really. But I must say when Uncle Fred left me this place, I wish he'd left some money to go with it. It's going to be hard, trying to keep it up.
Bob	Yes, I know. It was funny about the money, wasn't it? Everyone thought the old boy was really well off.
Stella	Well, we were all wrong. All he had was this house and a few bob in the bank. Poor Uncle Fred. I was very fond of him, you know.
Bob	I know, Stella. And he was fond of you, too. That's why he left you his house. Never mind, love. We'll make a go of it. You'll see! Now I'd better start washing up those dishes.

Scene 3 Cousin Ernest comes in. He is wearing a silk dressing gown, and yawning.

Ernest	Good morning, you two. Oh dear! Am I too late for breakfast?
Stella	Well, we were just clearing the tables. . . .
Ernest	Of course, I don't want to put you to any trouble, Stella. Don't worry about me.

After all, Uncle Fred didn't leave *me* anything so I suppose I don't matter.

Stella   It's all right. I'll do some breakfast for you. What do you want? Some tea and toast?

Ernest   Oh, nothing much. I don't eat a lot in the morning. A little orange juice before my cornflakes. Then a *tiny* bit of bacon and eggs. And perhaps just a few slices of toast and marmalade. That's all.

Bob   [*In a sarcastic voice*] Hardly enough to keep body and soul alive, is it?

Ernest   [*Glares at Bob*] Of course, if it's too much trouble ....

Stella   No, no. It's all right. I'll do it.

Ernest   I'll just go and dress while you cook it. Oh and Stella ...

Stella   Yes?

Ernest   I like my eggs done on both sides, please. See you in a minute. [*He goes out*]

Scene 4

Bob   How long is that little creep going to stay?

31

Stella	Not long, I hope. I don't know why he came here anyway. But he's always trying to make me feel bad about Uncle Fred's will.
Bob	I know. And you shouldn't. He hardly came near the old man except to try to borrow money.
Stella	He says Uncle Fred promised to leave everything to *him*.
Bob	Don't you believe it!
Stella	But what if it's true? It makes me feel rather guilty.
Bob	Rubbish! Anyway, you'd better do his ruddy bacon and eggs, I suppose. He'll be down in a minute. Then let's hope he goes out for the day. What was that funny noise in the kitchen?
Stella	Oh dear! I know what it was.
Bob	What?
Stella	Another bit of toast just hit the ceiling!

Scene 5 Later.

Ernest	That was a very good breakfast, Stella.
Stella	Glad you enjoyed it, Ernest. Er ... are

	you going back to London soon? I expect you have to get back to work.
Ernest	Oh, there's no hurry. I'm between jobs at the moment.
Stella	[*Her face falls*] Oh.
Ernest	Of course, if I'm in the way....
Stella	No, no. Of course not.
Ernest	I don't want to stay where I'm not wanted.
Stella	Not at all, Ernest. You are my cousin, after all.
Ernest	Yes, and Uncle Fred's nephew, don't forget.
Bob	[*In a low voice*] Here we go again!
Ernest	Oh yes! I've spent many happy hours in this house with dear old Uncle Fred. In fact, I almost look on this house as my second home.
Stella	Oh dear!
Ernest	What's the matter?
Stella	Did I say 'Oh dear' I meant 'Oh yes'.
Ernest	Well, I mustn't stay here talking. I'm going out for a stroll. It'll give me an appetite for lunch. So long!

Scene 6

Bob	Did you hear that? The greedy blighter is coming back for lunch!
Stella	And we don't have lunch in this house. We don't have time. After we've washed all the breakfast dishes ...
Bob	cleaned the house ...
Stella	made all the beds ...
Bob	done the shopping ...
Stella	it's time to start cooking dinner.
Bob	I know. You don't have to tell me. He'll have to go soon, Stella. I'll have a word with him.
Stella	No, Bob, please don't. He is my cousin after all.
Bob	I know. And he's Uncle Fred's nephew. As he keeps telling us. But that doesn't give him the right to stay here for ever. He's eating us out of house and home.
Stella	Yes, he does have a good appetite.
Bob	A good appetite! He's got a mouth like the Grand Canyon. All the food within miles of it just disappears.
Stella	[*Laughs*] Oh Bob, if he heard you!

Bob	I don't care. I'm fed up with him. And there's something else about him I don't like.
Stella	What's that?
Bob	I've seen him snooping around the house. Looking in drawers and opening cupboards.
Stella	Why would he do that?
Bob	I don't know, but I don't like it.
Stella	Are you sure, Bob?
Bob	Yes, Stella. I even found him poking about in the wood shed. I asked him what he was looking for and he made some silly excuse.
Stella	That is odd. I agree with you, Bob. We'd better keep an eye on Cousin Ernest.

[Mrs Baker *enters*]

Hello, Mrs Baker. Is anything wrong?

Mrs Baker	Not really, Mrs White. I don't want to complain but you know that cousin of yours? The one you call Ernest?
Bob	What's he done now?
Mrs Baker	We saw him coming out of our room

this morning. I expect he was helping you to clean the house. But would you ask him not to shift the furniture about next time he cleans? Everything was in the wrong place. Thanks very much. [*She goes out*]

Bob   Now do you believe me, Stella?

Stella   Helping to clean? Cousin Ernest!

Bob   That's the joke of the week. He's so lazy, he can hardly clean his own teeth!

Stella   But what was he doing in the Bakers' room?

Bob   I don't know but I don't like it. Your cousin Ernest is up to something and I'd like to know what it is.

Scene 7 Stella is cleaning one of the bedrooms. She hears strange noises coming from the attic upstairs.

Stella   What on earth is that noise? It seems to be coming from the attic. I'll call Bob and see what he thinks. Bob! Come here a minute please.

Bob   [*Comes in*] What is it, Stella?

Stella   Do you hear that noise?

Bob	What noise?
Stella	It was there a moment ago. Coming from the attic.
Bob	A scraping noise, you mean? It could be a mouse, I suppose.
Stella	Not exactly a scraping noise. It was more like puffing and grunting. More like a pig than a mouse.
Bob	Let's go and see.

[*They go to the attic and listen outside the door*]

You're right, Stella. It *is* a pig. And it's called Ernest.

[*He opens the door*]

Hello, Ernest. Why are you pulling those boxes about? We don't keep any food up here, you know.

Stella	Yes, what are you looking for? There's nothing up here but a load of junk.
Ernest	Oh, hello! Er ... I was just looking for ... er ... an old pair of wellingtons.
Bob	Wellingtons? In this weather? You must be crazy!

Stella	What for, Ernest?
Ernest	To do some gardening, of course!
Bob	Gardening? *You?* I bet you don't even know what a spade looks like.
Ernest	Oh, yes I do! And I thought I'd give you a hand while I'm here. I'll do some gardening for you.
Stella	That's very kind of you, Ernest. Er ... what were you thinking of doing in the garden?
Ernest	Oh, anything. I don't mind.
Bob	Well, you could mow the lawn....
Ernest	Oh, no! I hate pushing a heavy mower around. It's so tiring.
Stella	But it's an electric mower, Ernest.
Ernest	I don't like electricity; I might get an electric shock.
Bob	We can always hope.
Stella	Bob! Don't listen to him, Ernest. He's only joking. It's very kind of you to want to help us in the garden. What *do* you want to do?
Ernest	I think I'll do some weeding. See you both at dinner.

[Ernest *goes out. A little while later,*
Stella *looks out of the window*]

Stella   Bob!

Bob   Yes, love?

Stella   You know Ernest said he'd do some
          weeding?

Bob   Yes. So what?

Stella   Well, he has a strange way of doing it.
          All he's doing is digging a great big
          hole in the ground.

Bob   Good! If it's big enough he might fall in
          and end up in Australia!

          [*They both laugh*]

Scene 8   That evening. The dining room. The guests
are waiting for their meal.

Mrs P-S   What a pity the Ritz Hotel was full up
          this year.

Mr P-S   Yes. They always have such a nice class
          of people.

Mrs P-S   And lovely meals. Foreign, of course. I
          wonder what we're having tonight. [*To
          the* Bakers] Do you know?

Mrs Baker	Mrs White said it's fish and chips.
Mrs P-S	Dear me! How common!
Mr Baker	What's wrong with fish and chips? We like them very much.
Mr P-S	Yes, you would.
Mr Baker	Now what do you mean by that?
Mrs P-S	Don't answer him, Geoffrey. We mustn't sink to their level.
Mr P-S	We certainly won't come here again, my dear. Apart from the place, the other guests just aren't what we're used to.
Mrs P-S	Not our type at all.

[Bob *comes in with tray. So does* Stella]

Bob	Here we are, everyone. I hope you all like fish and chips.
Mrs Baker	Lovely! It's our favourite.
Mrs P-S	Better than nothing, I suppose.

[Bob *and* Stella *serve the guests.* Ernest *comes in*]

Ernest	Good evening. What's for dinner?
Bob	Nothing special tonight, Ernest. Only fish

40

and chips. I don't suppose it's fancy
enough for you.

Ernest   I'll do my best to eat it, though. After
all, I have to keep up my strength.

Bob   What for? Going for another stroll, are
you?

Ernest   Really Stella, I sometimes wonder how
you came to marry someone like Bob.
He has such a strange sense of humour.
Quite nasty at times.

Stella   That's enough, you two. Let everyone get
on with their dinner. Come on Bob, ours
is in the kitchen.

Scene 9 Next morning, Bob and Stella are clearing
the tables after breakfast. Mr Potter-Smith comes in.
He is very angry.

Mr P-S   Well, this really is the end!

Stella   What's the matter?

Mr P-S   The matter? This house is a wreck –
that's what's the matter. It isn't fit for
decent people to stay in.

Bob   Oh, come on! It's not as bad as that.

Mr P-S   Don't argue with me, young man. This

place is a ruin! My wife has just had a nasty accident.

Stella Oh dear! What kind of accident? Is she badly hurt?

Mr P-S It could have been a lot worse. But it was bad enough. My wife stepped on a loose floorboard in our bedroom. The other end jumped up and hit her on the nose.

Stella Oh dear! I *am* sorry.

Mr P-S Is that all you have to say? My wife could have been killed, but you don't care. People like you have no feelings. You may well hear from our lawyers. I think it's a disgrace! Now I'm going upstairs to pack. We're leaving this wreck of a house at once.

Bob Don't forget to settle your bill first.

[Mr Potter-Smith *goes out*]

Stella Oh dear! Now we're really in trouble.

Bob Don't worry, Stella. I'm sure the accident wasn't as bad as he says. These Potter-Smiths have done nothing but complain since they got here. That's the sort of people they are.

Stella	Yes, you're right. Still, we'll have to fix that loose floorboard.
Bob	Oh, yes. We don't want it to happen to another guest. I'll go and mend it as soon as the Potter-Smiths have gone.

Scene 10 A little later. *Stella* is alone. She is setting the tables. *Ernest* comes in.

Ernest	Good morning, Stella.
Stella	Good afternoon, Ernest.
Ernest	What are you doing?
Stella	Setting the table for tonight's dinner. I always do it early so I can get on with other jobs.
Ernest	Oh. What about my breakfast?
Stella	You were so late today that I put it in the oven to keep warm.
Ernest	Good! I'll go and get it. [*He gets the plate and sits down to eat*] Stella!
Stella	Yes?
Ernest	I'm a bit short of money at the moment. I don't suppose you could lend me ten pounds?

Stella	But I lent you five pounds last week.
Ernest	Yes, I know. It was very nice of you. But after all, dear old uncle Fred wouldn't like his nephew to starve.
Stella	I don't think there's much danger of that, Ernest. Not the way you eat.
Ernest	Well, what about the loan?
Stella	Sorry, Ernest. I can't afford to lend you any more money. Bob and I are hard up as it is. We can hardly manage to keep this place going.
	[Bob *and* Mr Baker *come in*. Bob *has a large suitcase*]
Bob	Hey, Stella! Look at this!
Stella	What is it?
Bob	An old suitcase. I found it under the loose floorboard. Someone had taken the nails out. Mr Baker helped me to get it out.
Stella	How odd! I wonder who it belonged to – and what's in it.
Bob	Let's open it and find out.
	[*He opens the case and they all gasp*]

Stella	Gosh! Look at all that money!
Bob	It's stuffed with banknotes.
Ernest	[*To himself*] So I was right! That's where he hid it – under the floorboards. If only I'd had more time to search.
Bob	So Uncle Fred wasn't poor after all.
Mr Baker	Look, Mr White. There's a letter in the case.
Bob	So there is. It's addressed to you, Stella. Go on – read it!
Stella	[*Opens the letter and reads*] My dear niece, I hope you find this suitcase. I hid it here because I don't like banks. You'll need money to keep this house going. By the way, don't let my nephew, Ernest, get his hands on any of it. He's a greedy young scoundrel. I was always lending him money. Don't make the same mistake. Good luck, my dear. Your loving uncle Fred.
Ernest	I knew it! I knew he must have hidden his money somewhere. The mean old skinflint!
Bob	[*Pretending to be shocked*] But Ernest! What about all those happy hours you spent with dear old Uncle Fred?

Ernest	Huh! Dear old uncle Fred, indeed! He was a greedy old miser. He wouldn't part with a penny if he could help it.
Stella	That's enough, Ernest. You'd better pack your bags and go now. I know why you came here.
Bob	You wanted to find Uncle Fred's money and keep it for yourself. That's why you were always searching the house.
Ernest	And I would have found it in the end. If only that silly woman hadn't had an accident with the floorboard.
Bob	Good old Mrs Potter-Smith!
Stella	Goodbye Ernest. I don't want to see you here again.
Ernest	But I haven't had my lunch yet.
Stella	Lunch? You must be joking. I'm not making any more meals for you. Now go and pack!
Bob	Good for you, Stella!
Ernest	Well, I must say you are a disappointment to me, Stella. You seem to forget we're cousins. After all, blood is thicker than water.
Stella	If you don't get out of here, we'll see

	just how thick your blood is. After I've spilled some of it.
Ernest	Oooh! Don't you dare touch me! I'm going to pack and get out of here. You're just as mean as that old miser, Uncle Fred.
Bob	Don't you mean 'dear old Uncle Fred'?
Ernest	No, I don't. And you're welcome to this old ruin of a house. I hope it falls about your ears!

[*He goes out and slams the door*]

| Bob | Dear me! What a change! What about all those happy hours he spent ... |
| Stella | In his second home? |

[*They laugh*]

Mr Baker	I hope you don't mind me saying so, but your cousin's a nasty piece of work.
Stella	I don't mind at all. I agree with you. What a relief to see him go!
Mr Baker	We leave tomorrow as well. It's the end of our holiday.
Stella	I hope you've enjoyed it.

Mr Baker	Oh, we have. We loved every minute of our stay here. It was so exciting. You never knew what would happen next.
Stella	What do you mean?
Mr Baker	Toast flying through the air, for one thing. You don't get that in every guest house. What a laugh we had.
Stella	You were very good to put up with all the things that went wrong. Next year, the house will be more comfortable.
Bob	Yes, we can afford to do our repairs now.
Mr Baker	Oh, we'll be back next year. Don't worry. We wouldn't miss bed and breakfast here for anything. [*Laughs, and 'puts on' a posh voice*] After all, you get such a nice class of people!